FOREWORD TO VOLUME 1

Because of today's increasing environmental destruction and urbanization, many people want to bring a bit of nature into their homes. Increasingly the method of choice is the terrarium. The fascinating chameleons call to mind dragons or dinosaurs and often are found on the wish lists of hobbyists. Unfortunately, only a few publications on keeping and breeding chameleons exist in the popular literature, and often potential hobbyists are informed that chameleons cannot be kept successfully in captivity. Only recently has captive-bred stock started to appear on dealer lists and in pet shops, making it possible for serious hobbyists to begin to consider chameleons as pets worth their investment in time and money.

The many peculiarities of chameleons, which extend far beyond their ability to change color and the "shooting tongue trick," are often unknown even to interested amateur herpetologists. This book, Volume 1, presents the fascinating world of chameleons, ancient but very specialized lizards that have managed to survive into modern times. Beyond that, Volume 2 is meant to provide guidance in setting up and maintaining terraria and in solving problems that come up. Special emphasis in this book has been placed on terrarium technology, because technology is the reason for greater successes in captivity.

W. KASTLE

Chamaeleo chamaeleon, the Common Chameleon.

These books make no claim to completeness, but rather are only intended to provide an overview of the commonly kept chameleon species and to familiarize the reader with these widely known, but in detail still quite unknown, dragons of our time.

Originally published in German under the title CHÄMALEONS *Drachen unserer Zeit* by Terrarien Bibliothek. Copyright 1989 by Herpetologischer Fachverlag.

SPECIES DESCRIPTIONS

In the following pages we will present descriptions as well as information on the care and breeding of a number of frequently kept species, including mating behavior and details of incubation or pregnancy where known.

ᨒ LIVEBEARING SPECIES ᨒ

Bradypodion pumilum
(Gmelin, 1789)
Cape Dwarf Chameleon

The Cape Dwarf Chameleon is one of the most popular species of chameleon kept in terraria. Although the species has been the object of numerous behavioral studies, breeding it over several generations seems to present big problems. *Bradypodion pumilum* is one of the long-lived chameleon species, living to to an age of up to five years.

An especially conspicuous character of *Bradypodion pumilum* is the large lobelike scales that form the gular (throat) crest and are largest

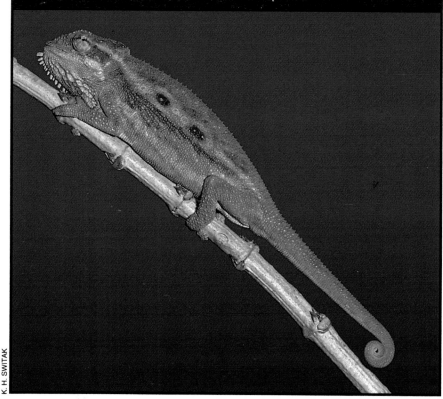

The Cape Dwarf Chameleon, *Bradypodion pumilum*. Note the row of enlarged rounded tubercles on the side, a feature of the species.

K. H. SWITAK

P. FREED

A small Cape Dwarf Chameleon, *Bradypodion pumilum*, exhibits a stress pattern. The blue and yellow only vaguely shown in this photo often are very obvious in adult males.

just before the tip of the snout. The casque (bony crest at the back of the head) is slightly raised and its sides are covered with large, convex tubercular scales. The dorsal crest consists of fairly regular conical tubercles that extend onto the tail. The body scaling is very irregular. The ground color is some shade of green, yellow, or brown. An elongated blue and pink to red stripe runs along each flank. Besides *Bradypodion pumilum*, many close relatives, such as *Bradypodion damaranum*, also are frequently kept and occasionally bred in captivity. The maximum total length is about 18 centimeters (7 inches).

Found in parts of South Africa and Namibia, these chameleons do not seem to be confined to a particular biotope there, but rather are attracted to all kinds of plants. Today the animals are particularly common in parks and gardens. The probable reason for this is that the owners water their gardens well and thereby create an ideal living space for insects, which in turn serve as food for the chameleons. The maximum daytime temperatures vary on average between 26 and 35°C (79 and 95°F). More detailed information is found in Burrage

(1973).

Interspecific aggressiveness is said to be weakly expressed, but nonetheless, the dominant lizard oppresses any others so much that only a single specimen should be kept in a terrarium. A pair of *Bradypodion pumilum transvaalensis* were, however, kept together until the female's death (at five years of age). During this period they reproduced six times.

For keeping, all of the usual terraria with large ventilation openings are suitable. The size for an adult animal should be at least 20 cm long x 30 cm deep x 50 cm high (8 x 12 x 20 inches). The furnishings can be simple: a few small plants on the bottom, many climbing branches, and a climbing plant. The daytime temperature should be between 25 and 28°C (77-82°F); in addition, a small spotlight for basking should always be present. Lowering the temperature at night by 10°C (about 15°F) is absolutely necessary for the well-being of the chameleon. *Bradypodion pumilum* can be kept outside the whole summer in large wire-mesh terraria.

All kinds of small insects are eaten. The favorite food is the maggots of the wax moth (wax worms), which are eaten in large numbers if provided. Because of their high fat content, however, wax worms should only be fed very sparingly.

Even when some rain falls in their living space, the animals still need a lot of water, and they must be given water every day. The best method is to spray the whole terrarium in the early morning. If the terrarium contains enough plants with suitable leaves on which the water droplets can collect, this is quite sufficient.

For breeding, the female is put in the terrarium with the male, whereupon the male usually begins to nod immediately. The female does not react until the male approaches. If she is ready to mate, she will not exhibit any direct reaction to the male. The male nods as he nears the female and mounts her from behind. Copulation lasts about 10 to 30 minutes.

About 90 to 105 days after mating, the 2 to 18 youngsters are born, usually in the morning hours. The offspring are very delicate. Rearing can take place singly or in groups in small terraria. Daily spraying of the rearing tank in the morning hours is necessary for the youngsters' survival. Without this water the baby chameleons would not even survive a day! The diet should be as varied as possible and should include springtails, *Drosophila*, and small crickets put loose in the rearing cage. The regular dusting of the food animals with a calcium-vitamin preparation is essential for supplying the youngsters with sufficient nutrients. During the first month of life the temperature should not exceed 25°C (77°F). Moreover, stuffy air absolutely must be avoided. The animals reach sexual maturity at about nine months of age.

reports have been published so far, even though various hobbyists have bred this species for generations. The animals have a life expectancy of about three years.

R. D. BARTLETT

Distinguishing the more than a dozen species of *Bradypodion* is a job for a specialist. This seems to be a Natal Midlands Dwarf Chameleon, *Bradypodion thamnobates*.

Chamaeleo ellioti
(Guenther, 1895)
Elliot's Chameleon

Chamaeleo ellioti is a rather nondescript chameleon that is frequently available (often under the name *C. bitaeniatus*). Unfortunately, no breeding

The casque of *Chamaeleo ellioti* is only slightly raised. The dorsal and gular crests consist of rather small, regular spiny scales. The body scaling is moderately irregular, usually with a single row of enlarged scales along the midside. The spectrum of colors includes almost all shades you could expect in a chameleon. The males have a green ground color with bright markings. Usually there is a white to blue-green stripe along the midsides over the row of enlarged scales. The females usually have a green, brown, or gray ground color with very fancy markings. The lizards vary greatly in color and pattern depending on locality. Some populations of *Chamaeleo ellioti* are just as beautifully patterned as the Carpet Chameleon. The black spots or stripes at the lower back edge of the gular pouch (throat sac), considered to be a typical character of the species, may be absent in many specimens. Heinecke and Graf informed us that they found populations in Zaire in which there were chameleons both with and without the black gular pouch pattern. The animals reach a maximum length of 22 centimeters (9 inches).

The closely related *Chamaeleo bitaeniatus* occurs in much the same range as Elliot's Chameleon and is similar in size and shape. Its

PHOTO COURTESY OF FOUR PAWS

Because chameleons take water by misting and by licking droplets off leaves and rocks, spray vitamins can be successfully added to their misting water.

scalation is much more mixed than in Elliot's, with large and small scales over much of the upper sides. The dorsal crest has alternating higher and lower scales, and the black on the gular (throat) pouch is absent. Often there are two rows of enlarged round scales on the sides rather than one. Elliot's Chameleon often has been considered a subspecies of *C. bitaeniatus* although the two species seem to occur together in some areas.

Chamaeleo ellioti inhabits all of eastern Central Africa. The species is found in Kenya, Tanzania, Uganda, Rwanda, Burundi, and Zaire at altitudes of 800 to 1800 meters (2640-5940 feet). It prefers bushes, high grass, and gardens, and often is present at a high population density. Heinecke (1989) considers the species to be a follower of civilization. The relative humidity in the range varies between 60 and 100 percent. The maximum daytime temperatures range from 25 to 28°C (77-82°F). The day-night variation is about 10°C (15°F).

Chamaeleo ellioti needs lots of

fresh air, so the best terraria are those with very large ventilation surfaces or even wood-framed terraria made completely of wire mesh. The minimum terrarium size for an adult animal is about 20 cm long x 30 cm deep x 50 cm high (8 x 12 x 20 inches). The daytime temperature should be about 25°C (77°F); in addition, a small spotlight must be

terrarium at least twice a day. The chameleons can be kept outside the whole summer.

Houseflies are the favorite food of *Chamaeleo ellioti*. They should be offered frequently, because the animals then become very lively and use all their skill to catch the flies. In addition, small crickets, whole small grasshoppers, small mealworms, flour moths, and

Elliot's Chameleon, *Chamaeleo ellioti,* usually is confused with the very similar Two-striped Chameleon, *C. bitaeniatus,* which is much more common in the hobby. Notice the uniform length of the spines in the crest, a good identification mark of this species.

turned on at times so that the animal can warm up. A day-night variation of about 8°C (12°F) is absolutely necessary. As an inhabitant of the open savannah, *Chamaeleo ellioti* needs good lighting, otherwise the animals will not be as active and will not exhibit their entire range of colors. An adequate relative humidity is achieved by spraying the whole

small wax moths are taken. The animals should be watered exclusively with sprayed water.

Interspecific aggressiveness is relatively slight in *Chamaeleo ellioti.* The animals are active the whole day and often exhibit a mood-dependent change in coloration. It is possible to keep a pair together in a large terrarium as long as the female is not pregnant. For mating, the female is placed in the terrarium with the male, whereupon the male immediately starts to nod. If the female is not ready to mate, she wards off the male in the usual chameleon manner. In so doing the female often displays a warning coloration of garish

fertilized.

After a gestation period of 100 to 160 days, the small chameleons are born. The adults mate again only two weeks later. It is no tragedy if this period after a birth is missed, because the females store semen in a sperm

Imported chameleons, especially those from Madagascar, often arrive without accurate names and may prove impossible to identify from a single stressed specimen that shows little in the way of color pattern. This stressed specimen might be a female or young male *Chamaeleo fischeri* from eastern Africa.

colors on a dark background. If the female is ready to mate, however, she does nothing at all at the sight of the male. The male approaches while nodding and mounts the female. Copulation lasts about 15 minutes. In the following days the animals should be put together repeatedly, so that as many eggs as possible are

receptacle. The litter size varies between 4 and 14 young. The young are hard to rear because they are very delicate. In the initial period the temperature should be about 22°C (72°F). After about a month it can be raised gradually to about 25°C (77°F). It is best to feed twice a day. The animals reach sexual maturity at about six to nine months of age.

Chamaeleo hoehnelii
(Steindachner, 1891)
Helmeted Chameleon

The Helmeted Chameleon numbers among the most frequently kept species, and there are a few hobbyists who

crest consists of large spiny scales that become smaller on the tail and finally disappear on its last third. The gular crest is composed of very long spiny scales. Two rows of greatly enlarged scaly plates can run on both sides of the body, and the entire scalation of the sides

R. WEDERICH

Just a few years ago the Veiled or Yemeni Chameleon, *Chamaeleo calyptratus*, was virtually unknown in the hobby. Today it is one of the most popular species, bred by hundreds of keepers but still expensive and desirable. Males have a fantastically high crest that distinguishes them from the Common Chameleon, *C. chamaeleo*, to which they are closely related.

have continued to breed it with constant success over five generations and more. Most specimens available are wild-caught, however. The maximum age is believed to be two to four years.

The most conspicuous features of *C. hoehnelii* are the tall casque and the small, scaly rostral process. The dorsal

is very mixed, with many large round scales surrounded by tiny ones. The ground color is almost always a shade of green. The animals turn dark only to warm up or when they are irritated. Furthermore, the coloration may also include white, yellow, red, light blue, brown, and black tones. The most commonly exhibited color

B. KAHL

A nice male Helmeted Chameleon, *Chamaeleo hoehnelii*, displays both a very high rounded casque and a small horn on the nose. Notice the heavy spines of the dorsal crest and the long spines on the gular (throat) crest.

pattern is made up of lozenge-shaped markings. The lizards vary greatly depending on locality, and several forms with quite different appearances have appeared on the market. The only reliable sex difference is the thickened base of the tail of the adult male. The maximum total length, which is reached by only a few forms of the Helmeted Chameleon, is 25 centimeters (10 inches); on average the animals only attain a size of 18 to 22 centimeters (7-9 inches). There is a very colorful subspecies of *Chamaeleo hoehnelii, Chamaeleo hoehnelii altaeelgonis.*

The range of *Chamaeleo hoehnelii* includes altitudes of 1200 to 2800 meters (3960-9240 feet) in East Africa. The subspecies *Chamaeleo hoehnelii altaeelgonis* inhabits altitudes of more than 3000 meters (9900 feet) on Mount Elgon. This large range and the tendency to occur mostly on isolated mountains make it clear why the animals show so much variation. *Chamaeleo*

W. KASTLE

Chamaeleo hoehnelii hoehnelii, the Helmeted Chameleon.

hoehnelii is found exclusively in bushes and undergrowth.

Helmeted Chameleons need terraria with a minimum size of 25 cm long x 30 cm deep x 50 cm high (10 x 12 x 20 inches). The animals need lots of fresh air, so the ventilation openings must be particularly large. Wire-mesh terraria or keeping the animals at liberty on a south-facing windowsill is especially suitable for this species. The temperature should be 25°C (77°F) during the day and should fall at least 10°C (15°F) at night. The relative humidity should be between 50 and 80 percent during the day and between 80 and 100 percent at night. This is achieved by spraying the whole terrarium at least three times a day. The animals have tolerated temperatures higher than 25°C only when the humidity was simultaneously very high. Keeping the animals outside throughout the summer is very beneficial.

Like other chameleons, this species eats all kinds of small food insects. Their favorites are

B. KAHL

The scalation of the head and casque of the Helmeted Chameleon, *Chamaeleo hoehnelii*, is especially coarse and quite distinctive for the species among common hobby chameleons.

houseflies, crickets, male green cockroaches, and small moths. The adults are very voracious. To keep them from getting too obese, they are only fed every other day. The animals meet their water requirement by licking up the spray water. This is quite sufficient if the terrarium is sprayed several times a day. At low relative humidity or when the chameleons are kept at liberty on the windowsill, the water requirement is greater, and you should give them water from a pipette.

For mating the female is put

As usual, coloration means very little in the Helmeted Chameleon, *Chamaeleo hoehnelii*, which can vary tremendously depending on mood and setting. This washed out specimen may just be reacting to the photographer's lights.

A. V. D. NIEUWENHUIZEN

in the terrarium with the male, which immediately starts nodding when he spots the female. If the female is not ready to breed, she darkens and also nods. When this happens the male usually breaks off the courtship. If the female is ready to breed, she barely reacts to the male and walks away slowly when approached. The male overtakes the female and mounts her from behind. Then he clasps the opening to her cloaca with his feet and "kneads" it several times. After that the female opens the cloaca and mating occurs. Copulation lasts about 10 to 30 minutes.

Females become even more voracious after mating. About two weeks before the birth of the little chameleons food intake decreases dramatically. The gestation period is four to six months. Birth usually takes place in late morning. The animals mate again about 40 to 50 days later. The litter size varies from 4 to 22 young. With this large number of young, it is essential to make sure that enough small insects are available to satisfy the hungry baby chameleons.

The temperature must not get too high when rearing the youngsters. For the first two months the daytime temperature should be 22°C

(72°F). With this species it is better to rear the young singly. The animals reach sexual maturity after about six months. Captive-bred

species on account of its appearance and its ease of keeping and breeding.

With the three horns on its snout (well-developed only in

R. D. BARTLETT

At first glance this three-horned chameleon might appear to be Jackson's Chameleon, but notice the oddly expanded casque and the narrow, spiny elements of the dorsal crest. This seems to be a related but different species. Remember that several chameleons have horns, so always look for other characters when making an identification.

specimens of the large variety first paired after 13 months.

Chamaeleo jacksonii
(Boulenger, 1896)
Jackson's Chameleon

Jackson's Chameleon, one of the three-horned species, is one of the most coveted chameleon

the males, unfortunately), *Chamaeleo jacksonii* is one of the most distinctive species. The middle horn is located directly above the tip of the snout and is curved slightly upward. The other two are at eye level and are pointed to the front. The body scaling is very variable in size and form, and the dorsal crest resembles a saw blade. The ground color is green to yellow brown with white or brown spots. Sometimes the coloration is reminiscent of "tree bark covered with lichen" (Klingelhoeffer). The total length of this East African lizard ranges up to 32 centimeters (13 inches). Females have either three small horns, only the middle one, or none at all. In the latter case the horns are suggested by conical scales. In case of doubt, however, males can be recognized by the thickened base of the tail. This species exhibits great geographic variability and the number of subspecies has yet to be clarified. *Chamaeleo jacksonii* is found in Kenya, Tanzania, and Uganda and can be found up to an altitude of 2000 meters (6600 feet). A more detailed discussion is found in Lin and Nelson (1981).

Chamaeleo jacksonii is not the only three-horned chameleon. There are a few other horned species, some with one horn, some with two, and a few with three or even four. Of these, two species that are occasionally imported, *C. oweni* and *C. johnstoni*, differ

An unusual female Jackson's Chameleon, *Chamaeleo jacksonii*, bearing a single large horn on the snout. Usually females have no horns or only small nubbins, but there is a lot of variation in this species depending on subspecies and locality as well as individuals.

R. D. BARTLETT

from *C. jacksonii* in having mostly regular small scales on the sides (rather than the very mixed scalation of *C. jacksonii*) and lacking the saw-toothed dorsal crest. Both also have lower casques than Jackson's Chameleon. In *C. johnstoni* the back edge of the casque is rounded, while in *C. oweni* it has two distinct lobes. Many male *C. oweni* have only a single horn.

Jackson's Chameleon is a species of the uplands that get abundant rainfall. Nairobi, Kenya, is located at an altitude of about 1800 meters (5940 feet) and the average morning temperature is about 11°C (52°F). In the afternoon the thermometer records a temperature of about 24°C (75°F).

Chamaeleo jacksonii is one of the few species in which a pair can be kept together. A prerequisite for this, however, is a very large, thickly planted enclosure. In general, it is better to keep the animals singly. The males are very intolerant of one another and must never be kept together in a terrarium.

Because the species comes from the highlands, the enclosure should be constructed accordingly. This

Facing Page: A fairly typical male Jackson's Chameleon, *Chamaeleo jacksonii*, in a very green color pattern. Notice the high but small casque with heavy conical scales marking it off and the broad bases of the elements of the dorsal crest. Photo: M. Panzella.

means that three sides should be of gauze and at most one of glass. The cover must also have a large gauze surface. Whenever possible, however, these animals should be kept at liberty on a planted windowsill. The terrarium must have a minimum size of 60 cm long x 50 cm deep x 80 cm high (24 x 20 x 32 inches). A small spotlight, depending on the size of the terrarium, ensures a daytime temperature of about 28°C (82°F). At night the temperature should fall to about 15°C (59°F) or lower. This large temperature variation is critical for increasing the life expectancy of *Chamaeleo jacksonii*. A relative humidity of 50 to 80 percent during the day and 80 to 100 percent at night promotes the lizard's well-being. This can be achieved by spraying the terrarium in the morning and evening.

The diet consists of practically all insects, from flies to grasshoppers, but slugs, snails, earthworms, and pinky mice also are eaten.

In the breeding season the female reacts with mild threats to visual contact with the male, but the threat behavior and bobbing soon stop. In this way the male recognizes the female's readiness to mate. A motionless resting female that turns lighter and lighter upon the male's approach also signals her readiness to breed. As the male approaches, her tail, which up until then had been rolled up, is slowly stretched out. The male comes from behind and clasps the base of the tail or the female's sides. The female now bends her back and raises her tail. Then the male clasps her nape and pulls himself onto her back. He seeks contact with her cloaca and inserts his hemipenis. The entire mating act lasts about 13 minutes, of which ten minutes alone are taken up by cloaca contact. The female breaks off the copulation by bobbing, turning darker, and moving forward. Further matings can take place in the following days. The female usually stays in breeding condition for 11 days, and in the event that mating still has not occurred may be breedable for up to 30 days.

Chamaeleo jacksonii is one of the livebearing species. About three and a half to six months after mating the female gives birth to the young. She stops eating for a fairly long time, sometimes several weeks, before the birth. In general, the birth of the 7 to 38 youngsters is announced by restlessness on the part of the female lasting one to two days. Finally the female passes the young, which are still enshrouded in the egg membranes, distributing them randomly about the terrarium. Birth usually occurs in the morning hours. Because of the sticky membrane, the shell-less eggs with the youngsters inside hang on the branches, though some eggs also fall to the bottom. By stretching its body,

Even without the horns, this female Jackson's Chameleon, *Chamaeleo jacksonii*, is readily identifiable by the shape and size of the casque, the details of the dorsal crest projections, and the mixed scalation of the sides. Photo: M. Smith.

the 5.5-centimeter (2-inch) baby chameleon weighing only 5.6 grams (a fifth of an ounce) breaks through the egg membrane and sticks its head out into the world for the first time. Soon after that it displays

its characteristic juvenile coloration, black with white triangular flecks. The entire act of birth can last between 32 and 225 minutes and is dependent on the number of young produced.

The young must be separated from the mother. At first the youngsters can be left together in groups, but it is safer to rear the animals singly. Even more so than with the adults, it is essential to make sure that the temperature does not get too high. The absolute maximum is 24°C (75°F) during the day. This temperature also should not be maintained constantly the whole day.

Rearing presents few problems. The youngsters are fed insects of appropriate size: small *Drosophila*, crickets, and other small insects. After a month the youngsters should

Look at chameleons with an eye to the scalation as well as obvious things like color patterns and horns. At first glance these two Madagascan chameleons are similar if you just look at the heads. However, notice that the *Chamaeleo balteatus* above has very even scalation on the sides (homogeneous scalation) and only small tubercles in the dorsal crest. The *Chamaeleo antimena* below has several sizes of scales and tubercles on the sides (heterogeneous or mixed scalation) and very broad-based projections in the dorsal crest. .

R. D. BARTLETT

have doubled their birth weight and after six months should be about twice as large as at the time of birth. They can reach sexual maturity at about nine months of age. The average maximum age is five to six and a half years, though one female lived to more than nine years of age.

⤳ EGG-LAYING SPECIES ⤳
Chamaeleo fischeri
Reichenow, 1895
Fischer's Chameleon

Chamaeleo fischeri reaches a length of just under 40 centimeters (16 inches), of which about half is taken up by the tail. Females are usually somewhat smaller. Although the markings of individual animals are quite variable, the ground color is always the same. The spectrum of colors of this species ranges from white, yellow, and all shades of green from light green to olive green, through gray and brown to black. The richly contrasting color structure of most male chameleons is seldom present. The most conspicuous character of this species is the pair of strongly compressed snout

Chamaeleo fischeri multituberculatus, a Fischer's Chameleon from the Usambara Mountains of Tanzania.

processes that can reach a length of up to 20 millimeters (almost an inch) in males, but which grow to only 10 millimeters in females or are absent entirely. The back of *Chamaeleo fischeri* is equipped with a crest of conical scales that in the male are irregularly distributed and extend to the tail, and which usually end on the first third of the body in females. The body scaling of these chameleons is relatively coarse and irregular. This species sometimes is put in the genus *Bradypodion*, but it differs considerably from the South African dwarf chameleons.

Fischer's Chameleon comes from East Africa (Tanzania and Kenya) and is found there in bushes and small trees on forest edges at altitudes of about 800 to 1700 meters (2640-5610 feet).

For keeping the animals, terraria starting with a size of 40 cm long x 40 cm deep x 60 cm high (16 x 16 x 24 inches) are suitable. A well-branched *Ficus benjamini* is particularly well-suited as a decoration. To ensure an adequate supply of fresh air, the sides and cover of the terrarium should consist is recommended. The light period is 12 to 14 hours. If at

K. H. SWITAK

Typical Kenyan Fischer's Chameleons, *Chamaeleo fischeri*, can be recognized by the combination of spinous dorsal crest, small flattened tubercles on the side (often appearing to be in squarish groups), and casque and rostral projection shape.

predominantly of gauze. A spotlight (up to 40 watts) installed in the enclosure will be used for basking. The temperatures in our terraria are maintained at 26 to 27°C (79-81°F) during the day and are allowed to fall by 6 to 10°C (about 10-15°F) at night. The relative humidity should be about 50 to 70 percent during the day; at night it will automatically rise somewhat because of the sinking temperature. To reach the desired value, spraying the whole terrarium each morning

all possible the animals should be offered direct, unfiltered sunlight. In any case, it is best to put the chameleons in outdoor terraria for a few hours on warm, sunny days.

Many different insects are suitable as food, including but not restricted to crickets, grasshoppers, cockroaches, wax moths and their larvae, king mealworms, and flour beetles, as well as pinky mice. A varied diet is essential, otherwise the food offered may be refused.

Water can be supplied to *Chamaeleo fischeri* by means of

an automatic drinker. In addition, the animals can also

spots the female, her ground color lightens and the white

R. D. BARTLETT

Close-up of a Fischer's Chameleon, *Chamaeleo fischeri*, showing just how heavy the rostral projection may be. Notice that the casque appears to be thin and rather smooth.

take up spray water daily. One or two drinks a week by means of a pipette are also quite sufficient.

When a female of *Chamaeleo fischeri* is ready for breeding, with some experience it is possible to recognize her condition on the basis of coloration alone. She exhibits a saturated, rich green color with a few light spots in the front half of the body and a bright yellow head. If the female is placed with a male, the male will begin with courtship immediately. As soon as he

pattern becomes clearly visible. Accompanied by vigorous nodding of the head, the male approaches the female, who either holds her position or moves forward slowly. The male now tries to mount the female from behind. This is followed by cloaca contact and copulation, which lasts about 10 to 15 minutes. Females that are not in breeding condition or are already pregnant turn blackish green and try to flee hastily when spotted by a male. Females stay in breeding condition for about seven to ten

days and will mate repeatedly during this time. In the following period the female will eat more food than usual.

The gestation period is 47 to 55 days. By the end of this time the eggs are already clearly visible. The female stops feeding and starts to dig in several places a few days before the eggs are laid, seeking a promising laying site. In our enclosures the substrate consists of a sand-peat mixture. If the conditions are suitable, she digs a burrow 15 to 20 centimeters (6-8 inches) deep at the end of which the eggs, which are about 12 x 8 millimeters (half an inch by a third of an inch), are laid. Finally, the female fills the hole in carefully and presses the substrate down with her feet.

embryonic development probably involves a pronounced day-night rhythm, 25 to 26°C (77-79°F) during the day and 12 to 14°C (54-57°F) at night. Only one youngster developed completely in the egg after a four-week incubation with a day-night rhythm in an incubator at a constant 25 to 26°C. Unfortunately, the animal was unable to leave the egg. Apparently the eggs, in the same way as *Brookesia* eggs, have to be incubated at room temperature.

It is not advisable to keep *Chamaeleo fischeri* with other reptiles or amphibians, because the animals are enthusiastic lizard-eaters.

Chamaeleo chamaeleon
(Linnaeus, 1758)
Common Chameleon

Of all the chameleon species, the Common or European Chameleon is probably the most familiar, at least as far as appearance of photos in books. This species is not readily available on the market and is considered threatened through much of its range. In fact, though it appears in almost all European terrarium literature, it barely enters Europe in the Iberian Peninsula and the Mediterranean Isles; it is much more typical of North Africa and the Middle East. (The Veiled or Yemeni Chameleon, *Chamaeleo calyptratus*, often has been considered a subspecies of the Common Chameleon and currently is one of the most

A young Common Chameleon, *Chamaeleo chamaeleon*, from Egypt. This wide-ranging lizard is one of the moderate-sized species and is quite short-lived, as are most chameleons. Once abundant from Spain through North Africa to India, it now is uncommon over much of its former range. Photo: P. Freed.

The clutch consists of 16 to 20 eggs, which unfortunately have never been matured successfully in our facilities. The trick for successful

W. SCHMIDT

The dry savannah or near-desert habitat of *Chamaeleo chamaeleon* in Tunisia. Animals from desert oases may lack any green in their color pattern.

reaches a total length of about 30 centimeters (12 inches), though the European animals usually only grow to a size of about 20 centimeters (8 inches). The body form is typical of chameleons, without any special features, such as horns. The casque is slightly raised in the rear and the scaling is virtually uniform, only the head having coarser scales. The coloration is very variable. As a ground color, the animals usually exhibit shades of green, yellow, gray, or brown. The lizards that occur around the oases of the Algerian Sahara no longer exhibit any hint of green in their coloration. Common Chameleons frequently have two longitudinal stripes consisting of white spots on the ground color. In addition, the animals often display dark or light flecks. The only dependable character for sex determination is the thickened base of the tail of the adult male.

Chamaeleo chamaeleon has a huge area of occurrence. The species inhabits all of North Africa, Israel, Jordan, Lebanon, and Syria, as well as southern

commercially bred large chameleons in the hobby.) These chameleons were already imported into northern Europe a century ago, and the first observations on keeping them were published by Fischer in 1882. Long-term captive breeding success has remained elusive until recent years, however. The only eggs came from imported pregnant females or from pairs that were caught and mated in the same year. Flower (1925) put the natural lifespan at about three and a half years. This seems realistic based on our observations. Unfortunately, no long-term observations have been made on this subject. Many chameleon species attain a much shorter life span in the wild than is often assumed.

The Common Chameleon

and western Asia Minor. In Europe the Common Chameleon is found in southern Portugal and Spain, on Sicily, Malta, and Crete, and in the southern Peloponnesians. Unfortunately, these populations are severely threatened by increasing habitat destruction. In Europe, the chameleons inhabit overgrown sand dunes and pine and eucalyptus forests. In North Africa they are found in the most diverse biotopes. We found the animals in open

A large adult Common Chamaeleon, *Chamaeleo chamaeleon*, showing a well-developed casque.

savannah, in open forests, and in oases. It was noteworthy that bodies of water were often in the immediate vicinity. The species inhabits altitudes of from 0 to 1750 meters (0-5775 feet). The inhabited sand dunes in Europe are characterized by their exposure to sun and wind, which is shown by the average temperature of 10°C (50°F) in January and 20 to 30°C (68-86°F) in July, and a proportionately high relative humidity of up to 84 percent in the morning and 40 to 50 percent during the day. On average there are 500 to 800 millimeters (20-32 inches) of rainfall a year.

As is true of most chameleons, interspecific aggressiveness is very pronounced in the Common Chameleon. In captivity these chameleons are highly incompatible even with other terrarium inhabitants, such as large *Phelsuma* day geckos, so that only single animals can be kept in a terrarium.

An important peculiarity of the European Chameleon is that the animals go into a kind of hibernation. They hide, sometimes even in small groups, in crevices or the like and spend the cold season there. When the temperatures are sufficiently high in the spring they emerge again.

All terraria with at least two ventilation surfaces are suitable. For adult animals terraria with a minimum size of 40 cm long x 40 cm deep x 70 cm high (16 x 16 x 28 inches) are adequate. Local sources of heat, in other words spotlights, absolutely must be present. The temperatures, corresponding to the season, should range between 23 and 30°C (73-86°F)

K. KNAACK

Common Chameleons, *Chamaeleo chamaeleon*, once were imported fairly often for the hobby, but today they are virtually unavailable. Much more common than the typical form shown here is the Veiled Chameleon, *Chamaeleo calyptratus*, once considered to be a subspecies and defined by having a much higher casque.

during the day and considerably lower at night. For the time of hibernation a temperature of 15°C (59°F) is recommended. An adequate relative humidity is achieved by spraying the terrarium thoroughly in the morning.

The Common Chameleon eats all of the usual food insects. Depending on provenance, the animals may show a preference for certain foods, such as grasshoppers or cockroaches. With time most of the chameleons get used to taking water from a water bowl. Almost all drink water from spraying. Otherwise the animals are given water twice a week from a pipette.

Like all reptiles that are subject to an annual periodic reproductive cycle, the synchronicity of the sexes (meaning that both the male and the female are simultaneously in breeding condition) is a requirement for breeding. In some reptiles the animals are ready to breed immediately after the end of a sufficient period of hibernation. Unfortunately, it is not so simple with the European Chameleon. Instead, the animals do not enter breeding condition until the second half of the year. For a successful breeding in the terrarium, this raises the question of what triggers readiness to breed, including maturation of eggs and sperm. Apparently it is the decrease in the natural day length. This means that the terrarium lighting must be regulated such that up to June 21 the light period increases and then decreases after that. We would like to request that a *Chamaeleo chamaeleon* keeper who has the opportunity to care for the animals independently of the natural light conditions would communicate to us his or her experiences with respect to the reproductive activity of the chameleons.

For mating, the female is put in the terrarium with the male. If the female is not ready to mate, she shows this through a warning coloration of bright pale spots on a dark background when the male spots her. If the male still approaches, he is immediately threatened and attacked in the usual manner. In *Chamaeleo chamaeleon* the male recognizes the female's readiness to mate because she refrains from any kind of intimidation behavior and continues to walk slowly away. Copulation lasts about 12 to 20 minutes. In our experience the briefer copulations lasting about a minute so often cited in the literature are actually interrupted mating attempts that are not sufficient to fertilize a female. This is also true of other chameleons.

The female buries the eggs about 40 to 60 days after copulation. The clutch size varies between 14 and 46 eggs. The size of the freshly laid eggs is about 11 x 17 millimeters (about half an inch by two-thirds of an inch).

The question of where and how to incubate the eggs must be addressed. The simplest method consists of bedding the eggs in slightly moist vermiculite and incubating them at a constant 27 to 29°C (81-84°F). With this method the little chameleons hatch after about 190 to 240 days. Unfortunately, the joy in having a clutch of little chameleons is tempered somewhat after three months when it is determined that all are females. We have yet to hear of a single case of males bred in captivity! More experimentation is obviously in order here. We would like to make a few suggestions for the incubation period: 1) higher temperatures during the entire period of incubation; 2) a cool phase, analogous to *Chamaeleo lateralis*. Experiments with uniformly low temperatures during the entire period of incubation have failed.

The rearing of the young is relatively straight-forward. They should be kept singly in small terraria at a temperature of 25°C (77°F) and a nocturnal decrease of about 6°C (10°F).

If you want to place your chameleons into hibernation, feeding must be halted a week beforehand so that the intestines can empty. The terrarium is simply placed in a basement with a temperature of about 15°C (59°F). You must not forget to put a dish with fresh water in the terrarium and replace it as needed. The animals should be brought out of hibernation after about two months.

Chamaeleo dilepis (Leach, 1819) **Flap-necked Chameleon**

This chameleon species formerly was imported frequently but currently is not commonly seen. On first sight the most noticeable feature of this chameleon is the low casque with a deeply indented flap at the back over the nape. The animal can spread this flap like an elephant spreads its ears, reaching a maximum angle of 90°. The flap is covered with large scales of about equal size. The throat (gular), ventral (belly), and dorsal crests are clearly visible. On the flank there is a light stripe extending from the chin or the shoulder. The ground color is green. The maximum size is reported as

K. PAYSAN

A typical Flap-necked Chameleon, *Chamaeleo dilepis*, one of the more slender and unornamented species. The main identifying character of the species rests in the divided flap behind the casque.

just under 38 centimeters (15 inches). Males are smaller than females and have an ankle spur. In the event that the sex determination is still uncertain, the thickened base of the tail of the male is, as usual, diagnostic.

In the forested regions and wooded savannahs of tropical and southern Africa, the Flap-necked Chameleon probably is one of the most abundant chameleons. Several different climatic conditions prevail over its large range, so the hobbyist should endeavor to determine the origin of any purchased specimen. Here we will use the keeping and breeding of the South African form as an example, but remember that chameleons from other parts of the range may require different incubation temperatures and probably different cycles of day and night temperatures as well. These chameleons absolutely must be kept singly, because they are extremely quarrelsome. When Flap-necked Chameleons are kept together, they always bite each other, which can lead to serious injuries. Even without bodily contact it must be expected that at the impetuous approach of a male, the female will fall into a kind of akinesis, turn totally black, and recover only after a fairly long time.

For ventilation, one side and the top of the terrarium should consist of wire mesh. The ideal location for the terrarium is a sunny place, which, however, must also provide the animal the opportunity to seek out shade. A spotlight and fluorescent tubes help to produce suitable temperatures and lighting conditions for the chameleon. The substrate should consist of a 10-centimeter (4-inch) layer of a soil-sand mixture. During the day the temperature should be between 25 and 32°C (77-90°F), and it should be allowed to drop to 18 to 22°C (65-72°F) at night. A relative humidity of 50 to 60 percent during the day

J. VIERKE

Usually obvious in most patterns of the Flap-necked Chameleon, *Chamaeleo dilepis*, is a white line very low on the sides. Though often broken or short, it typically is present.

and 80 to 90 percent at night is appropriate. Spraying the terrarium in the morning and if necessary in the evening helps to achieve these values.

All of the usual kinds of food can be offered: wax moth larvae, crickets, grasshoppers, flies, spiders, and moths. The chameleons meet their drinking requirement from the spraying of the plants. It is also worthwhile to see if the chameleons will drink from a dish. In addition, they should be given water twice a week from a pipette.

At mating time, when the female exhibits yellow spots on the green ground color, the sexes are put together. The female reacts either with slow flight or she remains perched on her branch and threatens mildly. The male approaches very impatiently; often he does not court at all. Copulation takes place in the usual manner and lasts a total of about 20 minutes.

About 30 to 50 days after

Though simple in appearance at first glance, the Flap-neck has many distinguishing features if you know what to look for. *Chamaeleo dilepis* is one of the few common chameleons in which the spines of the gular crest continue almost without interruption along the middle of the belly to well past midbody. Notice also how even all the scalation is, both on the sides and on the limbs. Photo above: J. Bridges; below: R. D. Bartlett.

K. LUCAS

From above, you can see the heavy pointed tubercles that outline the crests on the head and to the back help form the low casque of *Chamaeleo dilepis*.

incubator. The young hatch after about ten months and are about 37 millimeters (1.5 inches) long, the tail making up half of the length. The body length can double within two months, and with optimal diet and care, the young can reach a length of 10 centimeters (4 inches) after three months and 15 centimeters (6 inches) after seven months. After about a year the little chameleons are fully grown and hence sexually mature. Young Flap-necked Chameleons must be reared singly. A daytime maximum temperature of 25°C (77°F) should not be exceeded. As with all young chameleons, an adequate supply of vitamins and minerals must be provided.

mating, the female lays between 19 and 58 eggs. The eggs should be put on moist vermiculite at 28°C (82°F) in an

The "other" three-horned chameleon common in the hobby, *Chamaeleo johnstoni*, the Smooth Three-horned Chameleon, often is confused with Jackson's Chameleon.

R. D. BARTLETT

R. D. BARTLETT

A female Smooth Three-horned Chameleon, *Chamaeleo johnstoni*, is an interesting lizard but not an exciting one. Notice the absence of the high, saw-toothed crest typical of Jackson's Chameleon.

Chamaeleo johnstoni
(Boulenger, 1901)
Smooth Three-horned Chameleon

With a length of about 30 centimeters (12 inches), *Chamaeleo johnstoni* is one of the medium-sized chameleon species. Less than half of the total length falls to the tail. Because *Chamaeleo johnstoni* is one of the horned species, the appearance of the male is quite impressive. The three yellowish, concentrically ringed horns reach a length of 16 to 30 millimeters (about 0.6 to 1.2 inches); the rostral (nose) horn is curved slightly upward and is somewhat thicker than the two preorbital horns. In females the horns are totally absent. The coloration of both sexes is quite variable. Males exhibit a light green ground color broken up by turquoise bands and scattered ocher-yellow spots. The gular pouch also is turquoise, and the edges of the mouth are ocher-yellow. The ground color of the female is a light olive green, covered with numerous small black spots, which are also found in small numbers in the male. Shades of light blue are found in the female only on the head; the gular pouch is orange-yellow. The eyes are reddish brown. The body scaling consists of large granular scales, among which are interspersed small, flat, tubercular scales. The saw-toothed crest of the other common three-horned chameleon, *Chamaeleo jacksonii*, is absent, so the dorsal crest is smooth.

This chameleon is found living in the Central African uplands at altitudes of 1000 to 2400 meters (3300-7920 feet). The strong winds that are almost always present there (Heinecke, oral communication) force the animals to use their claw-equipped grasping feet to hold on tightly. They live on trees at a height of several meters. In our terraria the animals show a considerably stronger grip than do other chameleon species.

The aggressiveness of *Chamaeleo johnstoni* is also very pronounced. Any hand that gets close to them is immediately threatened with a wide-open mouth and loud hissing. If the presumed enemy seems unimpressed, the chameleons often simply let themselves fall to the bottom, where they roll themselves into a ball. In so doing the mouth remains open and threat

Shades of light blue sometimes mark the head of a female Smooth Three-horned Chameleon, *Chamaeleo johnstoni*, and yellow spots often are found on the lips of both sexes.

K. H. SWITAK

continues. Even youngsters exhibit this behavior.

The terrarium for this species must be constructed and furnished in a way that corresponds to the natural habitat. The minimum size is 40 cm long x 40 cm deep x 80 cm high (16 x 16 x 32 inches). To satisfy the lizard's need for fresh air, at least two sides of the enclosure should consist mostly of wire mesh. Climbing branches (not too thin) and a green plant make up the furnishings. The substrate consists of a sand-peat-soil mixture. A spotlight for basking is not absolutely necessary; nevertheless, a site must be present in the enclosure in which the daytime temperature reaches 25 to 26°C (77-79°F). A nocturnal fall in temperature of about 10°C (15°F) is absolutely necessary. The relative humidity should be 50 to 70 percent, somewhat higher at night. The animals are given water twice a week; as a supplement, they can take up spray water daily. *Chamaeleo johnstoni* eats all of the usual food animals. The food requirement is very small.

The climatic conditions in the homeland of *Chamaeleo johnstoni*—the highlands of Central Africa—make it seem likely that the species is ovoviviparous. This is also claimed in the literature (Kaestle, 1972). In fact, however, *Chamaeleo johnstoni* lays 12 to 16 eggs, each about 20 x 12 millimeters (0.8 x 0.5 inch), an impressive size in comparison to other species of similar build. The eggs can be incubated in plastic containers filled with damp vermiculite at constant temperatures of 22 to 23°C (72-73°F). The youngsters hatch after a period of development of about 100 days and are about 75 millimeters (3 inches) long. They have an olive-green to pale green ground color with a pattern of black spots, which strongly resembles the coloration of the adult female. Very conspicuous is a bright white stripe on each side of the head that extends from near the angle of the mouth across the upper and lower jaws. In the course of growth, this stripe becomes paler. After about eight weeks the youngsters have grown to a length of 80 to 85 millimeters (3.2-3.4 inches) in females and 82 to 92 millimeters (3.2-3.6 inches) in males. Four weeks after hatching, the sexes can be distinguished by the growth of the horns in the males.

The rearing of *Chamaeleo johnstoni* is relatively easy at temperatures of 22 to 25°C (72-77°F) during the day and 16°C (60°F) at night, with a relative humidity of 60 to 80 percent. The babies will feed on small crickets and *Drosophila* a few

Facing Page: This large, rather stout-looking female *Chamaeleo johnstoni* shows the scalation features of the species clearly. Notice that there are few large tubercles on the side of the body, another distinguishing feature from Jackson's Chameleon. Photo: M. Panzella.

P. FREED

A male Mountain Chameleon, *Chamaeleo montium*, is a very odd yet beautiful lizard. The two horns are distinctive among hobby species, but when combined with the high back and the crest on the tail you produce a unique chameleon.

hours after hatching.

Chamaeleo montium
(Buchholz, 1874)
Mountain Chameleon

The Mountain Chameleon is a very attractive and distinctive chameleon that has never been common in terraria. The most conspicuous features of the male are the two horns on the tip of the snout and the sail on the back and tail. In adult animals the horns reach a length of almost 20 millimeters (0.8 inch). The casque is flat, slightly raised, and rounded. The scales are in part small and flat, in part large, round, and flat. The chameleons exhibit a pale to dark green ground color. A broad, paler band, often yellowish green, running from the back diagonally to the rear often is present. Females have small conical scales in place of the horns and they lack the dorsal and caudal sails. Furthermore, they are smaller than the males. At a total length of almost 25 centimeters (10 inches), this chameleon is quite impressive.

The Mountain Chameleon occurs only in Cameroon at altitudes of 500 to 1200 meters (1650-3960 feet). It is very abundant on Mount Cameroon and even lives right on the sides of the roads, for example in Buea. It is found in bushes and trees, as well as in the elephant grass. Though hard to find when it rains and during the day, it is easy to find in the morning and late afternoon, since at these times it likes to sun itself in open places. A high relative humidity prevails in the natural habitats of this chameleon.

If you try to grasp a female Mountain Chameleon with your hand, she normally will try to bite. If not, she will simply drop from the branch and then disappear like a flash in the undergrowth or simply lie motionless in the grass. The males can attack with their horns. Nonetheless, we are unaware of any cases in which the chameleons have injured each other with their horns. Females also fight with each other. Therefore, Mountain Chameleons should always be kept singly. Yet in nature we have also found pairs sunning themselves only 10 centimeters (4 inches) apart. The males relatively often are found on the ground, where they sometimes dig holes and crawl inside, leaving only their heads sticking out.

The terrarium for the Mountain Chameleon should consist of wire mesh on only one side and the cover, for the animals need high humidity. A relative humidity of 100 percent at night and 70 percent during the day would be desirable. It is also necessary to spray the terrarium three times a day.

A female Mountain Chameleon, *Chamaeleo montium*, is a plain green animal at first glance. However, notice the large round plates on the sides that help distinguish this species.

R. D. BARTLETT

Temperatures of 23 to 27°C (73-81°F) during the day and 18°C (65°F) at night suit them best. Avoid high temperatures. An automatic drinker is recommended.

They accept all kinds of foods. Our animals receive crickets, grasshoppers, flies, wax moths, and cockroaches. Adults can be fed every other day; pregnant females and youngsters must of course receive food daily. The animals drink from the leaves after the terrarium is sprayed or they wait under the drinker for drops of water.

If the female is not willing to mate, she indicates this to the male through her dull dark green color with even darker bands and by bobbing up and down. In the terrarium she will move quite quickly as far away from the male as possible. If, however, the female is ready to breed—which can be the case starting after she is seven months old—she exhibits a bright pale or dark green coloration. In addition, she remains quietly perched or only wanders off from her perch very slowly. Courting males are light green on the head with yellow-green blotches on the body; the large, round scales on the sides turn light blue. They approach the female while bobbing the head. Copulation occurs in the usual manner for chameleons and lasts about 4 to 20 minutes. It is best to place the mating pair together for several consecutive days until the

A fully developed male Mountain Chameleon in all its sail-tail glory. Unfortunately, Mountain Chameleons are not often imported and seldom are bred in captivity, but the species is available to the determined keeper.

R. S. SIMMONS

A baby Mountain Chameleon, *Chamaeleo montium*, already displays the large plates on the side. This two-week-old young will mature in another seven to 12 months.

female refuses the male.

The female lays her five to eight eggs two months after mating. The egg form can be highly variable, elongated in one clutch and oval in the next. The substrate should be about 10 centimeters (4 inches) deep and consist of a mixture of sand and soil that must be moist, but not wet. The eggs are placed in a clear plastic container filled with vermiculite. In an incubator set at 25 or 26°C (77-79°F), with a nocturnal cooling to 16°C (60°F), it takes about 14 weeks for the young to hatch. The hatchlings have a total length of 5.5 to 6 centimeters (about 2-2.5 inches). They are reared individually in modified coffee cans with a coarse substrate and a plant. A few small branches make the miniature terrarium habitable for the youngster. At first they should be fed fruitflies that are well dusted with minerals. Later the food increases in size along with the youngsters. It is necessary to spray three times a day. In addition, attempts should be made repeatedly to try to get the youngsters to take water from a pipette. The sexes can be distinguished after a short time, because the horns

R. D. BARTLETT

There should never be a problem identifying Mountain Chameleons, *Chamaeleo montium*, because the species has so many distinctive features. The young male or female above may lack horns and crests but still displays the same round plates on the side as the brilliant male below.

P. FREED

Chamaeleo minor, an uncommon Madagascan chameleon.

K. TAMM

If it did not come from the Comores, *Chamaeleo cephalolepis* might be confused with *C. dilepis* at first glance because of the row of spines running down the belly. The casque is entirely different, however. Notice the white stripe on the side of this male.

develop early in the males. At temperatures of 22 to 25°C (72-77°F) during the day and 18°C (65°F) at night, the young develop well and reach sexual maturity after 7 to 12 months.

Chamaeleo cephalolepis
(Guenther, 1880)
Comoro Flap-nose Chameleon

Chamaeleo cephalolepis is one of the two known chameleon species from the Comoro Islands, the other species being the very closely related *Chamaeleo polleni*. It reaches a maximum length of 18 centimeters (7 inches) in males and 13 centimeters (5 inches) in females, though most males do not grow larger than 16.5 centimeters (5.6 inches). The tail makes up about 50 to 60 percent of the total length. The ground color is a rich, bright, light green; in males a white lateral stripe is present, but it rarely occurs in females. When irritated *Chamaeleo cephalolepis* also exhibits shades of yellow and dark green. The body scaling is uniform. On the sides of the casque there are large tubercular scales, these continuing onto the snout. In males these scales extend about 2 millimeters past the tip of the snout, but in females they do not reach the tip. Moreover, males are easily recognized by the clearly thickened base of the tail.

Chamaeleo cephalolepis inhabits the island of Moroni in the Comores, where a hot and humid coastal climate prevails. It is found there in dense shrubbery and bushes. The relative humidity ranges from 60 to 100 percent. The daytime temperatures are 26 to 30°C (79-86°F), with a nocturnal cooling of 6 to 8°C (about 10-14°F).

This is a relatively lively chameleon species with a strongly expressed aggressiveness. Even considerably larger would-be enemies are attacked if they get too close. After warming up in the morning under a spotlight, the animals wander through the terrarium almost the whole day in search of food. Suitable enclosures would start at a size of 20 cm long x 20 cm deep x 30 cm high (8 x 8 x 12 inches) and should be furnished with plenty of climbing branches as well as a *Ficus benjamini.* Ventilation openings should be present in one side and in the cover of the terrarium. A 25-watt spotlight serves for warming up the animals and for bringing the enclosure to the desired temperature of 26 to 30°C (79-86°F). Adequate humidity is achieved by spraying the whole enclosure twice a day. Fluorescent tubes are used to light the enclosure 12 to 14 hours a day. A soil-peat mixture serves as a substrate.

The lizards are fed small crickets, cockroaches, wax moths and their larvae, and *Drosophila. Chamaeleo cephalolepis* is especially fond of houseflies. Give them water once a week; in addition, they can take up spray water daily.

Chamaeleo cephalolepis has been bred many times under the following conditions. So as not to miss opportunities when adult females are in breeding condition, they are placed with a male every three days. The male will begin courting immediately and approach the female while nodding his head vigorously. If the female is not in breeding condition, she takes on a distinct warning coloration consisting of dark green spots over the entire body and a blackish green color on the head. If the male approaches anyway, he is immediately bitten. If the female is in breeding condition, she perches quietly as the male approaches. Copulation itself proceeds as previously described for the other species and lasts only five minutes. To obtain many fertilized eggs, the animals should be put together as often as possible.

The gestation period is 33 to 45 days; the pregnant female eats up to the last day. The four to seven eggs (about 12 x 8 millimeters, a half inch by a third of an inch) are laid at the end of a self-excavated nest burrow that is carefully filled in by the female. The eggs are placed in air-tight plastic boxes filled with moist vermiculite and then incubated in a standard incubator at a temperature of 26 to 28°C (79-82°F).

The young, which are only 48 millimeters (almost 2 inches) long, hatch after an extremely long incubation of 244 to 310 days. They exhibit a dirty white to beige coloration with green spots, and only begin to take on the coloration of the adults after about four months. The growth of the youngsters is very slow in comparison to most other species, and after 180 days they measure only 80 millimeters (a bit over 3 inches).

The young are reared in small terraria or plastic containers with dimensions of about 10 cm long x 10 cm deep x 15 cm high (4 x 4 x 6 inches). These are furnished with small, thin branches and a climbing plant. The temperature during the day should be no higher than 26°C (79°F), and a nocturnal cooling of about 8°C (about 14°F) is strongly recommended. The enclosure is sprayed briefly once a day.

The youngsters are highly susceptible to shedding problems, so they must be inspected for skin remnants after each shed (especially on

A male Carpet Chameleon, *Chamaeleo lateralis*. In this species males are much less colorful than the females.

R. D. BARTLETT

R. D. BARTLETT

Though female Carpet Chameleons, *Chamaeleo lateralis*, can assume a multitude of colors depending on mood and activity, they usually show a bright stripe down the middle of the side.

the feet), since otherwise the blood supply to the affected limbs could be cut off, causing them to swell up and die. The young chameleons reach sexual maturity after about a year.

Chamaeleo lateralis
(Gray, 1831)
Carpet or Jewel Chameleon

On account of its bright coloration and its lively behavior, the Carpet Chameleon is one of the jewels of our terraria. The common name refers to the bright, intricate patterns of a Persian carpet. This species is easy to keep and breed in captivity. In the wild the chameleons live to the age of one year. With appropriate keeping and care, in captivity the lizards easily reach an age of two to three years. The females, however, stop reproducing after the fourth to sixth clutch and live for another year after that.

The Carpet Chameleon has a roof-shaped, slightly raised casque. The body scaling is uniform, with scattered platelike scales. The most distinctive feature is the markings. Typical of the markings is the lateral stripe, which is always present, even in freshly hatched young. Also characteristic are the oval spots on the sides of the body that vary considerably from individual to individual. The

This male *Chamaeleo lateralis* has the thin white stripe typical of the species and the bright green color typical of its sex.

ground color of the animals can be gray, brown, or green. The lateral stripe and spots always stand out to some extent. Most often the animals have very variable, colorful markings with a bright white lateral stripe. In general, females are more colorful than males. The most conspicuous colors are displayed by females that are in breeding condition or carrying eggs. These chameleons can reach a total length of 25 centimeters (10 inches). No subspecies are known, although the animals vary greatly in size and coloration depending on the locality. After the fiftieth day of life, it is easy to distinguish the sexes by the male's greatly thickened tail base. With some experience it is possible to identify the sex by the coloration starting on the 14th day of life.

Chamaeleo lateralis is native to all of Madagascar, with the exception of the north and the northwest. It inhabits diverse vegetation zones, including rainforest, arid forest, and wet grass savannah. It is very common in hedges and meadows. The Madagascan climate is characterized by a pronounced summer-winter rhythm. The daily maximum temperature in summer is 26 to 30°C (79-86°F) and 18 to 24°C (65-75°F) in winter. The day-night variation is on average about 12°C (almost 20°F).

As might be expected, this is a very aggressive species. It can only be kept singly, never with conspecifics or other chameleon species, though they have lived peacefully with *Phelsuma* and more typical geckos.

The Carpet Chameleon should be kept in a terrarium with dimensions of 30 cm long x 40 cm deep x 60 cm high (12 x 16 x 24 inches). The terrarium is ventilated by means of small gratings on the front and in the cover so that the air cannot get stuffy. To light the terrarium, 50-watt mercury-vapor lamps should be used because they provide the necessary light and heat. The temperatures range during the day between 23 and 32°C (73-90°F) and at night between 15 and 25°C (59-77°F). The temperature must not exceed 32°C (90°F). The relative humidity should always lie between 60 and 100 percent. This is achieved by spraying the entire terrarium twice a day.

This is a big chameleon with a very big appetite. It is best to feed a varied diet daily. We have never heard of obesity in this species. The Carpet Chameleon eats crickets, *Drosophila*, houseflies, small migratory locusts, flour moths, and wax moths. Only when they are very hungry do the animals eat mealworms, the usual brown cockroaches, and baby mice. The absolute favorite food is the green cockroach. The lizards should have the opportunity to take up spray water every day in the form of drops. In addition, they can be given water from a pipette twice a week.

When a male spots a female,

Female Carpet Chameleons, *Chamaeleo lateralis*, usually display at least traces of large oval rings regularly spaced over the pale midside stripe. These sometimes can be detected in males as well.

R. D. BARTLETT

he immediately runs to her while nodding his head. If the female is not ready to breed, she threatens the male and bites him as soon as he comes closer. Usually the males are not influenced by this display in the least, and they only give up after the second or third failure. Unfortunately, some females are particularly aggressive and cause serious injury to the male. Therefore, it is essential always to be present during mating attempts. Some males, in their excitement, forget the nodding and immediately rush to the female. If the female is ready to breed, which is easily determined by the greatly decreased aggressiveness and the coloration, she does not threaten the male as he approaches. She merely tries to walk away slowly, but is overtaken by the male. The animals copulate, the male climbing sideways on top of the female and bringing the

PHOTO COURTESY ENERGY SAVERS

Carpet Chameleons and many other species like hot, bright lights. Your pet shop sells a variety of lights to fit all your needs.

opening of his cloaca under the female's. Copulation lasts about 10 to 20 minutes. After mating, the female drives the male off again. Sometimes the male tries to bite the female after mating.

The females lay their eggs after a gestation period of 30 to 52 days. In the terrarium they make no attempt to bury their eggs, but rather simply scatter them on the bottom of the terrarium. To prevent accidents, it is important that no food animals remain in the terrarium. In the wild the females lay four to five clutches of 4 to 23 eggs from November 15 to April 15, laying them in self-excavated holes in the soil that are 10 centimeters (4 inches) deep (Blanc & Blanc, 1971). The females are ready to

Facing Page: There is no doubt why hobbyists consider *Chamaeleo lateralis* to be one of the premium chameleons and hard to beat when it comes to color. Photo: M. Panzella.

mate again two weeks after the eggs are laid. The eggs must be removed immediately from the terrarium and transferred to a standard incubation container filled with slightly moist vermiculite. A cool phase is the trigger for the development of the eggs. In our experience, the following temperature schedule always led to the hatching of the little chameleons in a virtually equal sex ratio: 25°C (77°F) during the first 45 days, then 40 days at 10 to 15°C (50-59°F) in a cool basement, then the temperature should be held at 27 to 28°C (81-82°F) until hatching. The babies hatch about 100 days after the end of the cool phase. With our chameleons the incubation period was between 154 and 378 days. The rearing of the young is unproblematic. At temperatures of about 25°C (77°F) the growth rate is tremendous. The animals are sexually mature after four months.

Chamaeleo pardalis
(Cuvier, 1829)
Panther Chameleon

The Panther Chameleon is one of the more frequently bred chameleon species today. One of the authors bred 105 youngsters just in 1988. Because of its size and hardiness, this species is especially recommended for the not so experienced chameleon keeper. In captivity the animals have a lifespan of about four years; in the wild they only live about two years.

The dorsal crest consists of large, closely spaced spiny scales that become increasingly smaller to the rear. The gular crest also is made up of spiny scales. The snout is enlarged to the sides and front by large scales. Within its large range, so many different color varieties have evolved that a description would be beyond the scope of this book. The most frequently kept form is the color variety from Nosy Bé. Juveniles are gray or brown. They do not lose the juvenile coloration until they are six to nine months old, when they become sexually mature. All the lizards have a lateral stripe made up of large oval spots of different sizes, the colors of which always stand out somewhat from the rest of the body. Adult males are easy to distinguish by the thickened base of the tail. In addition, they usually are larger and more conspicuously colored than the females. Males can reach a size of 52 centimeters (21 inches) and females a size of 35 centimeters (14 inches), but usually the animals are somewhat smaller.

The range encompasses northern and eastern Madagascar, the nearby islands of Nosy Bé and Nosy Boraha, the region around Fort Dauphin, and the islands of Mauritius and Réunion. These chameleons are found only in coastal areas with a hot, humid climate. Throughout the entire range there is a summer-winter

The Panther Chameleon, *Chamaeleo pardalis*, is one of the largest and most hardy chameleons available to the average hobbyist. It often is bred in captivity, a necessity since most specimens only live three years.

rhythm, with an extensive rainy season in the southern summer from November to March. The average daily temperatures are 22 to 28°C (72-82°F), and the maximum daily temperatures in the southern summer reach about 25 to 40°C (77-104°F); the day-night difference is about 6°C (about 10°F) on average. The relative humidity varies between 70 and 100 percent. Panther Chameleons do not seem to prefer a particular biotope. They live in trees, in bushes, and in palm trees and often are found in the vicinity of human settlements, in gardens, and on the edges of fields. They avoid forests. When forests are cleared within the range, the Panther Chameleon colonizes these places. The other chameleon species that had lived there are displaced by civilization, but this species prospers with the changes caused by man.

Chamaeleo pardalis is a very lively and nervous chameleon species. The aggressiveness is very strongly expressed, so the animals must be kept singly.

Because of the liveliness of the species, the terrarium must not be too small. Sufficient for a full-grown male is a cage about 50 cm long x 50 cm deep x 120 cm high (20 x 20 x 48 inches). A female can be kept in a smaller terrarium, about 40 cm long x 50 cm deep x 80 cm high (16 x 20 x 32 inches), but a layer of substrate at least 15 centimeters (6 inches) deep must be present for egg-laying. *Chamaeleo pardalis* is a sun worshiper, which is why it absolutely must receive sufficient illumination. The daytime temperature should be about 28°C (82°F). A grating on the front or the side and another on top provide adequate ventilation so that the air does not get stuffy. The Panther Chameleon is particularly well suited for keeping at liberty in a windowsill or full-size greenhouse.

Chamaeleo pardalis eats all of the usual food insects and baby mice. It is essential to make sure that food intake is regular. An often groundless "hunger strike" is sometimes ended by offering a green food animal. Caution is advised, however, because the females in particular like to hunt small lizards. The animals are given water twice a week with a pipette. In addition, they can take up spray water every day. Most of the chameleons also

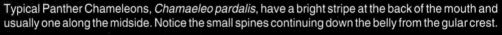

Typical Panther Chameleons, *Chamaeleo pardalis*, have a bright stripe at the back of the mouth and usually one along the midside. Notice the small spines continuing down the belly from the gular crest.

R. D. BARTLETT

R. D. BARTLETT

Male Panther Chameleons, *Chamaeleo pardalis*, have small flattened rostral projections but otherwise are much like females in both pattern and scalation.

learn quite quickly to drink from a water dish.

For mating, the female is placed in the terrarium with the male or the animals can be allowed to run at liberty in a greenhouse. When the male spots the female, he lightens his ground color and the striped markings stand out particularly brightly. He approaches while bobbing and presents his flattened side to the female. If the female is not ready to breed, when she sees the male she immediately opens her mouth wide and charges in the male's direction. After that the male usually breaks off his attempt to approach. If the female is ready to breed, which is easy to determine by her behavior toward the keeper because she fails to show any aggressive behavior, she does not display any defensive behavior toward the male. While the male approaches slowly, the female tries to run away or hide. The male approaches while nodding his head and then climbs on top of the female from behind. The female is completely motionless during this time and presses herself flat to the object on which she happens to be perched. When the male has clamped all four feet onto the female's body or legs, he makes jerky movements, after which the female raises her tail about

3 centimeters (a bit over an inch) so the male can place his tail under hers. Copulation lasts about 10 minutes.

The females remain receptive to breeding for about three days, but after that they behave particularly aggressively and exhibit a ravenous appetite. The sexes can only be put together for breeding and kept together only for the duration of breeding. Even then it is important to be present so as to be able to prevent fights. Young males, in particular, are quite rough and inexperienced, so it can easily happen that the female starts a fight. The flight behavior of the Panther Chameleon is particularly striking—it tries to elude its attacker by making numerous aimless jumps.

About 31 to 45 days after mating, the female lays her 12 to 46 eggs at the end of a self-excavated passage reaching to the bottom of the terrarium. Afterward she closes the passage carefully. About two weeks later the female is again ready to breed, which is apparent in the change in coloration and the decreased aggressiveness. About ten days after the eggs are laid, when the female is in good condition again, try to put her and the male together every third day.

The eggs must be removed from the terrarium immediately. They are incubated at 28°C (82°F) in slightly moist vermiculite. The young hatch after 159 to 323 days. They are no trouble to rear, but growth is strongly dependent on an adequate supply of water, nutritious food, and proper temperatures. At first the temperature should be 25°C (77°F), but after two months it can be raised to 28°C (82°F).

❧ GROUND CHAMELEONS ❧
Brookesia minima
(Boettger, 1893)
Tiny Ground Chameleon

Brookesia minima is the smallest known chameleon species and one of the smallest reptiles. It has been bred

Many different colors and patterns of the Panther Chameleon, *Chamaeleo pardalis*, exist in Madagascar, but they all agree in having the bright stripe on the side and usually the white stripe over the lips. Photo: K. H. Switak.

successfully without removing the eggs from the terrarium and without special methods of incubation. The lifespan is two years.

The body form is cylindrical, the head not clearly set off from the body. The snout is very short and curves steeply upward. The scaling is irregular. Running over the whole body are wavy, meandering longitudinal rows of small streaks that are especially coarse on the top of the head. Along either side of the back runs a row of small spines that gradually breaks up on the tail. The ground color is highly variable; the animals can take on shades of green, brown, and gray. The markings often consist of longitudinal stripes. Rarely the animals have a plain

W. SCHMIDT

The smallest chameleon, and one of the smallest lizards, is the Tiny Ground Chameleon, *Brookesia minima*.

or braided coloration. The forehead is often bright beige. Our largest female reached 33 millimeters (1.3 inches), the largest male 28 millimeters (1.1 inches). Newly hatched youngsters are 14.5 to 15.5 millimeters (0.6 inch) long. The males are easy to distinguish under the magnifying glass by the thickened base of the tail. Moreover, they are smaller and considerably flatter in build than the females.

Brookesia minima occurs only on Nosy Bé, a small island located northwest of Madagascar. The Tiny Ground Chameleons inhabit the leaf layer of the small remnants of primeval forests. There they prefer light undergrowth on hard ground. On Nosy Bé a hot and humid coastal climate prevails. The same temperatures and humidity should be present as for the care of *Chamaeleo pardalis*. It is important to note that in the natural habitat the

temperatures on the ground are lower and the humidity is higher than is apparent from the climatic data.

Interspecific aggressiveness is only weakly developed. For example, only occasional threat displays were observed between males. Nevertheless, in no case may several males be kept together. On the other hand, groups consisting of one male and several females have gotten along well in a "large" terrarium. The youngsters are also very quarrelsome with one another, so they should be reared individually in the smallest terraria.

Despite their tiny size, these chameleons need a roomy terrarium. A terrarium 40 centimeters (16 inches) on a side has proved to be suitable for a group of one adult male and two adult females. The terrarium is lighted with a fluorescent tube. Spotlights and direct sunlight are avoided by the lizards. The required relative humidity of 80 to 100 percent is achieved through very frequent spraying of the entire terrarium and through small ventilation openings. The temperatures should range between 23 and 25°C (73-77°F) during the day, but 25°C (77°F) should not be exceeded. The day-night decrease should amount to 6°C (about 10°F). The substrate should consist of garden soil or loam. A medium containing expanded polystyrene or similar plastic spheres should never be used—

the tongues of the lizards stick to the plastic and the animals choke to death. A layer of leaves or something similar (such as pieces of bark or cork mounded on the surface) must always be present. The remaining furnishing of the terrarium consists of many thin branches and a few small climbing plants.

Probably the most difficult topic in the care of *Brookesia minima* is the diet. Adult animals eat small *Drosophila*, aphids, whiteflies, springtails, and any other tiny insects that could be found in a terrarium. It is better not to feed small crickets, because after a few days these could view the chameleons as food and could also prey on the eggs. All food animals, because of the rather one-sided diet, must be dusted frequently with small amounts of a vitamin-mineral supplement. The chameleons meet their water requirement exclusively by licking up spray water. Only young aphids and springtails, which must always be present in large numbers in the rearing enclosure, are suitable as food for the young.

The courtship behavior of *Brookesia minima* is very pronounced and differs greatly from that of the other chameleon species. The male courts the female with head bobbing and jerky movements. If the female is not ready to breed, she makes several vigorous lateral movements, whereupon the male breaks off

R. D. BARTLETT

Brookesia minima is one of the more plainly scaled ground chameleons, with only low "horns" over the eyes and a few large tubercles along the backbone. Many species are very spiny and most bizarre tiny dragons.

courtship. If the female is ready to breed, however, she runs though the terrarium the whole day with the male. After a period of intense courtship the male climbs on the female's back and lets himself be carried around the terrarium. This behavior closely resembles clasping in frogs and toads. Copulation always takes place at the end of the day, in late evening or at night. The male pushes his tail under the female's, without angling it downward. The actual copulation lasts up to half an hour. The question of what purpose the bright spot on the forehead serves is still unexplained. It is possible that it is used for interspecific communication or even to attract insects. Because of the tiny size of the animals, for breeding they must be kept in pairs or in groups of one male and two females.

The freshly laid eggs have a size of about 2.5 x 1.5 millimeters (0.1 x 0.07 inch). It should be obvious that it would be very difficult to find the eggs in the terrarium. Therefore, it is absolutely necessary to set up the substrate conditions in the terrarium so that the eggs will develop without our intervention. The most important requirement is a moisture trap in the substrate, so the animals can seek out a site with suitable substrate moisture for egg-laying. To achieve this we place a double bottom at an angle in the terrarium, upon which a layer of garden soil about 3 centimeters (a bit over an inch) deep is placed. About four months elapse between an observed mating and the resultant hatching. The offspring that hatch in the terrarium must be removed immediately and reared individually in the smallest terraria. The daytime temperature should be about 22°C (72°F). It is not possible to rear several youngsters together, even in larger terraria. The interspecific aggressiveness is more pronounced than in the adults. Every day the small terraria are sprayed twice and, if necessary, more springtails are added.

Brookesia stumpffi
(Boettger, 1894)
Dead Leaf Chameleon

Brookesia stumpffi is one of the more frequently kept and bred species of ground chameleon today. We ourselves are already breeding them in the second generation. The chameleons reach a maximum age of three to four years. This is one of the armored ground chameleons. It has a cylindrical body covered with small spiny scales. Arranged in pairs along the back are large, flat spines that point to the sides. The top of the head is slightly arched and equipped with fairly large spines on the occiput and above the eyes. From a distance the animal looks like a dead leaf. The ground color usually is brown, but can also be reddish or even olive brown, and can lighten or darken depending on mood. During the breeding season the males exhibit a pattern of lichenous markings with shades of brown, gray, and green. *Brookesia stumpffi* reaches a maximum size of almost 10 centimeters (4 inches).

The Dead Leaf Chameleon inhabits the north and northwest of Madagascar as well as the nearby island of Nosy Bé. The habitat includes the leaf layer and the low shrubs of the primeval forests, but this species also colonizes abandoned coffee plantations. A hot and humid coastal climate generally prevails in its range. Daytime temperatures average 23 to 28°C (73-82°F). The daily maximum values in the southern summer are extremely high, but the temperatures in the niche occupied by the chameleons are lower.

Brookesia stumpffi should be kept individually in terraria with dimensions of at least 30 centimeters long x 30 centimeters deep x 30 centimeters high (12 x 12 x 12 inches). The ventilation opening should not be too large, so that the relative humidity does not fall too much, but the air must not be stuffy either. The temperature should range between 23 and 28°C (73-82°F) during the day and 17 to 20°C (63-68°F) at night. It is necessary to spray the terrarium several times a day. In the furnishing of the terrarium it is absolutely necessary to provide many protected hiding places in the form of an imitation leaf layer of crumbled sheets of cork.

This little chameleon eats all of the usual food insects up to a size of about 1 centimeter (half an inch or so). It is especially fond of houseflies and freshly hatched grasshoppers. The most favorable feeding time is the morning, when the animals move actively through the terrarium and search for food.

K. PAYSAN

The Dead Leaf Chameleon, *Brookesia stumpffi*, deserves its name. In many ways they are the Madagascan equivalents of the African genus *Rhampholeon*, also leaf mimics.

The chameleons should receive as much food as they want. Leftover food animals should never be left in the terrarium, because they prey on eggs. It requires some observation to determine the proper amount to feed. In every terrarium a small dish with small pieces of cuttlebone or other calcium supplement should be available to cover the calcium requirement, because the lizards have been observed taking up calcium repeatedly. The water requirement is met exclusively by licking up spray water, but many also are very fond of drinking from leaf axils, such as those of bromeliads.

The interspecific aggressiveness is very pronounced, as has been shown recently by experiments. For example, a conspecific is not greeted by a neutral nodding as in other chameleons, but rather by immediately opening the mouth wide and swaying back and forth. Only after some time do the males at least check the sex of the other chameleon. If the other is also a male, serious fights can occur in which dominance is determined. If the other chameleon is recognized as a female, which can take hours under certain circumstances, the male ceases all threat behavior. Usually it loses the normal brown coloration and assumes a lichenous pattern. While bobbing his head and jerking his body, he follows the female. After a short time he recognizes whether or not the female is ready to mate. In the latter case he breaks off the courtship. No new threat behavior patterns could be observed subsequently. Females that were not in breeding condition were repeatedly observed to wag their heads. Usually the males chase only the females in breeding coloration. Then the animals spend the whole day perched next to each other. The male attempts repeatedly to copulate with the female, but his efforts are not successful until toward evening. Before the actual copulation the male runs around the female while twitching his body and nodding his head, always maintaining body contact. Finally he mounts from behind. Copulation lasts about ten minutes.

The female lays two to five eggs about 40 days after mating. She usually stays exclusively on the bottom a few days before laying the eggs and searches for the ideal laying site. About two weeks after egg-laying, many keepers put the female together with a male in a very large terrarium equipped with numerous hiding places and keep the animals together until mating is observed or it is apparent that the female is pregnant again. Mating usually takes place 20 to 40 days after egg-laying. The eggs must be removed immediately from the terrarium and transferred to a small container filled with very moist vermiculite. Good hatching results are achieved when the eggs are matured at fluctuating temperatures between 18 and 22°C (65-72°F). The young hatch after about 50 to 60 days. Eggs matured at temperatures warmer than 25°C (77°F) do not develop completely. It was noteworthy that we were only able to rear offspring to maturity with an incubation period of more than 45 days. The rearing of the youngsters is unproblematic. As a first food, springtails (about one week old) are indispensable. In addition, however, aphids and *Drosophila* should also be offered. The ideal rearing temperature is about 22°C (72°F); temperatures of 28°C (82°F) or more have proved to be fatal.

ACKNOWLEDGMENTS

We wish to give special thanks to Mrs. Ursel Friederich, Dipl. Biol., Stuttgart, for numerous suggestions and much information, and for the support that helped to ensure realization of the manuscript, as well as to Dr. W. Boehme, Bonn, for reviewing and correcting the manuscript.

We would also like to thank everyone who, through sharing information with us, contributed to the success of this book. We would like to single out the following individuals in alphabetical order: K. Assmann, Muenster; A. Graf, Beimerstetten; S. Heinecke, Wuppertal; F. W. Henkel, Bergkamen; W. Kunstek, CW Kerkrade; R. Leptien, Alveslohe; K. Liebel, Herne; V. Mueller, Soest; M. v. Niekisch, Stuttgart; J. Peitschmann, Aalen; B. Seume, Soest; H. Simon, Dreieich; K. Steffen, Kamen; R. Stockey, Hagen; R. Zobel, Herne.

Last but not least, we thank Mrs. G. Schmidt for the preparation of the original manuscript.

BIBLIOGRAPHY

Altevogt, R. & R. Altevogt (1954) "Studien zur Kinematik der Chamäleonzunge," *Z. vergl. Physiol.*, 36: 66-77.

Angel, F. (1942) *Les Lézards de Madagascar.* Memoires de L'académie, Malagache, XXXVI.

Atsatt, S. R. (1953) "Storage of sperm in the female Chameleon, *Microsaura pumila pumila*," *Copeia*, 1953: 59.

Benzien, J. (1954) "Einiges über *Chamaeleon fischeri matschiei*," *DATZ*, 7(11): 295-298.

Blanc, F. (1970a) "Contribution á l'etude de la croissance postembryonnaire de *Chamaeleo lateralis* Gray, 1831," *Ann. Univ. Madagascar, Sér. Sci.*, 7: 321-343.

Blanc, F. (1970b) "Le cycle reproducteur chez la femelle de *Chamaeleo lateralis* Gray, 1831," *Ann. Univ. Madagascar, Sér. Sci.*, 7: 345-358.

Blanc, F. & Ch. Blanc (1971) "Élévage de *Chamaeleo lateralis*," *C. R. Soc. Herp. France*, 1: 30-34.

BNA (1987) *Das neue Artenschutzrecht.* BNA-Handbuch, Köln.

Böhme, W. (1982) "Ein neues Chamäleon aus Tanzania, mit Bemerkungen über Mimese bei Echsen," *Bonn. zool. Beitr.*, 33, Heft 2-4: 349-361.

Böhme, W. & C. Klaver (1981) "Zur innerartlichen Gliederung und zur Artgeschichte von *Chamaeleo quadricornis*," *Amphibia-Reptilia*, 3/4: 313-328.

Bourgat, R. M. (1968) "Comportement de la femelle de *Chamaeleo pardalis* Cuvier, 1829 aprés l'accouplement," *Bull. Soc. zool. Fr.*, 93: 355-356.

Bourgat, R. M. (1970) "Recherches écologiques et biologiques sur le *Chamaeleo pardalis* Cuvier, 1829 de l'ile de le Réunion et de Madagascar," *Bull. Soc. zool. Fr.*, 95: 259-269.

Bourgat, R. M. (1971) "Vie en captivité des caméléons malgaches," *Aquarama*, 5: 41-44.

Brygoo, E. R. (1971) "Reptiles Sauriens Chamaeleonidae. Genre *Chamaeleo*," *Faune de Madagascar*, 33: 1-318. Orstom et CNRS, Paris.

Brygoo, E. R. (1978) "Reptiles Sauriens Chamaeleonidae. Genre *Brookesia* et complément pour la genre *Chamaeleo*," *Faune de Madagascar*, 47: 1-73. Orstom et CNRS, Paris.

Burrage, B. R. (1973) "Comparative ecology and behaviour of *Chamaeleo pumilus pumilus* and *Chamaeleo namaquensis* (Sauria: Chamaeleonidae)," *Ann. S. Afr. Mus.*, 61: 1-158.

Bustard, H. R. (1958) "Use of horns by *Chamaeleo jacksonii*," *Br. J. Herpet.*, 1958: 105-107.

Cooper, J. E. & O. F. Jackson (eds.) (1981) *Diseases of the Reptilia*, Vol. 1 & 2. Academic Press, London.

Daiss, S. (1978) "Haltung und Aufzucht von *Chamaeleo hoehnelii*," *DATZ*, Stuttgart, 31: 64-67.

Dischner, H. (1958) "Zur Wirkungsweise der Zunge bei Chamäleons," *Natur und Volk*, 9: 320-324.

Eggers, J. (1963) "*Chamaeleo basiliscus*: Terrarienaufzucht in zweiter Generation," *DATZ*, 16: 242-246.

Fischer, J. v. (1882) "Das Chamäleon (*Chamaeleo vulgaris*), sein Fang und Versand, seine Haltung und seine-Fortpflanzung in der Gefangenschaft," *Zool. Garten*, 23: 70-82.

Fitzsimons, V. F. (1943) "The lizards of South Africa," *Transvaal Mus. Mem.*, 1: 1-528.

Francke, H. (1963, 1964) "Probleme der Haltung und Zucht von Chamäleons," *DATZ*, 16: 344-346. 374-377; *DATZ*, 17: 23-25, 54-56.

Friederich, U. (1985) "Beobachtungen an *Rhampholeon kerstenii kerstenii* im Terrarium," *Salamandra, Bonn*, 21(1): 40-45.

Friederich, U. & W. Volland (1981) *Futtertierzuchten.* Verlag Eugen Ulmer, Stuttgart.

Frisch, O.v. (1962) "Zur Biologie des Zwergchamäleons (*Microsaurus pumilus*)," *Z. Tierpsychol.*, 19: 276-289.

Heinecke, S. (1989) MS. "Reise ins Kivu," *DATZ*.

Hillenius, D. (1959) "The differentiation within the genus *Chamaeleo* Laurenti, 1768," *Beaufortia*,

8(89): 1-92.

Hillenius, D. (1963) "Comparative cytology: aid and new complications in chamaeleon-taxonomy," *Beaufortia*, 9(108): 201-218.

Ippen, R., H-D. Schröder & K. Elze (1985) *Handbuch der Zootierkrankheiten. Band 1. Reptilien.* Akademie Verlag, Berlin.

Isenbügel, E. & W. Frank (1985) *Heimtierkrankheiten.* Verlag Eugen Ulmer, Stuttgart.

Kästle, W. (1967) "Soziale Verhaltensweisen von Chamäleonen aus der *pumilus bitaeniatus*-Gruppe," *Z. Tierpsychol.*, 24: 313-341.

Kästle, W. (1967) "Soziale Verhaltensweisen von Chamäleonen aus der *pumilus bitaeniatus*-Gruppe," *Z. Tierpsychol.*, 24: 313-341.

Kästle, W. (1972) *Echsen im Terrarium.* Franckh-sche Verlagshandlung, Stuttgart.

Kästle, W. (1982) "Schwarz vor Zorn, Farbwechsel bei Chamäleons," *Aquarien Magazin*, Stuttgart.

Klaver, Ch. J. J. (1981) "Chamaeleonidae. *Chamaeleo chamaeleon* (Linnaeus, 1758), Gemeines oder gewöhnliches Chamäleon," *Handbuch der Reptilien und Amphibien Europas*, 217-238.

Klingelhöffer, W. (1957) *Terrarienkunde III. Teil: Echsen.* Stuttgart.

Krintler, K. (1977) "Nachwuchs bei Helmchamäleon, "*DATZ*, 30: 352-354.

Leptien, R. (1988) "Haltung und Nachzucht von *Furcifer polleni*," *Salamandra, Bonn,* 242/3): 81-86.

Linn, J. & C. E. Nelson (1981) "Comparative Reproductive Biology of Two Sympatric Lizards," *Amph.-Rep.*, 3/4: 287-311.

Loveridge, A. (1957) "Checklist of the Reptiles and Amphibians of East Africa," *Bulletin of the Museum of Comparative Zoology*, Cambridge, 109: 153-360.

Matz, G. & M. Vanderhaege (1980) *BLV Terrarienführer.* BLV-Verlagsgesellschaft, München, Wien, Zürich.

Mertens, R. (1946) "Die Warn-und Drohreaktionen der Reptilien," *Abh. senckenb. naturforsch. Ges.*, 471: 1-108.

Mertens, R. (1951) "*Brookesia stumpffi*, ein madagass. Zwergchamäleon, in Gefangenschaft," *DATZ*, 4: 329-330.

Mertens, R. (1966) "Chamaeleonidae," *Das Tierreich,* 83: 1-37.

Nietzke, G. (1978) *Die Terrarientiere 1 und 2.* Verlag Eugen Ulmer, Stuttgart.

Oeser, R. (1961) "Chamäleonpflege I-III," *DATZ*, 14: 53-56, 91-84, 116-117.

Parcher, St. R. (1974) "Observations of the natural histories of six Malagasy Chamaeleontidae," *Z. Tierpsychol.*, 34: 500-523.

Petzold, H. G. (1973) "Das Geheimnis der Chamäleonzunge," *Forschende Kamera, Urania*, 49(11): 14-16.

Petzold, H. G. (1982) "Aufgaben und Probleme bei der erforschung der Lebensäußerungen der Niederen Ammionten (Reptilien)," *Berliner Tierpark buch, Nr. 38, Nachdruck aus Milu*, 5(4/5): 485-786.

Podloucky, R. (1987) "Das neue Artenschutzrecht und seine Folgen für die Amphibien-und Reptilienhaltung," *Herpetofauna*, 9(50): 9-16.

Ravet J. (1948) "Atlas climatographique de Madagascar," *Publ. Serv. météorologique Madagascar, Antananarivo*, 10: 1-96.

Schifter, H. (1965) "Erfahrungen mit einem Pantherchamäleon," *Zool. Garten*, 30 (3/4): 179-181.

Schifter, H. (1971) "Familie Chamäleons," *In: Grzimeks Tierleben*, VI: 229-245.

Schmidt, W. (1984) "Springschwanzzuchten. Der kleine Tip," *Sauria*, 6(3): 11.

Schmidt, W. (1985) "*Chamaeleo lateralis*," *Beilage zur Sauria, Amph./Rept.-Kartei:* 41-42 Berlin W. 7 (40)

Schmidt, W. (1986a) "Brookesia stumpffi," *Beilage zur Sauria, Amph./Rept.-Kartei:* 41-42 Berlin W. 8(2).

Schmidt, W. (1986b) "Über die Haltung und Zucht von *Chamaeleo lateralis* (Gray, 1831)," *Salamandra, Bonn,* 22(⅔): 105-112.

Schmidt, W. (1987) "Bemerkungen Uuber das Pantherchamäleon," *Herpetofauna*, 9 (47): 21-24.

Schmidt, W. (1988) "Zeitigungsversuche mit Eiern des madagassischen Chamäleons *Furcifer lateralis* (Gray, 1831)," *Salamandra, Bonn,* 24(⅔) 182-183.

Schmidt, W., F. W. Henkel & W. Böhme (1989) "Zur Haltung und Fortpflanzungsbiologie von *Brookesia stumpffi* (Boettger, 1894)," *Salamandra, Bonn,* 25(1).

Schmidt, W. & K. Tamm (1987) "Nachzucht vom Teppichchamäleon," *DATZ*, 40(12): 561-563.

Schmidt, W. & K. Tamm (1988a) "Nachtrag zu Bemerkungen über das Pantherchamäleon," *Herpetofauna*, 10(52): 11.

Schmidt, W. & K. Tamm (1988b) "*Furcifer pardalis,*" *Beilage zur Sauria, Amph./Rept.-Kartei:* 101-104 Berlin W. 10(1).

Schmidt, W. & H. Simon (1988a) "Die kleinste bekannte Chamäleonart der Welt, *Brookesia minima*," *DATZ*, 41(5): 90.

Schmidt, W. & H. Simon (1988b) "*Brookesia minima,*" *Beilage zur Sauria, Amph./Rept.-Kartei:* 121-124 Berlin W. 10(4).

Schuster, M. (1979) Experimentelle Untersuchungen zum Beute-fang, Kampfund Fortpflanzungsverhalten von *Chamaeleo jacksonii.* Dissertation. Münster.

Schuster, M. (1984) "Zum fortpflanzungsbiologischen Verhalten von *Chamaeleo jacksonii* Boulenger, 1896," *Salamandra, Bonn,* 20 (2/3): 88-100.

Schuster, D. & M. Schuster, (1980) "Haltung und Zucht von *Chamaeleon jacksonii* bis zur zweiten Generation," *Zool. Garten N. F.*, Leipzig, 50:49-51.

Schwenk, K. (1985) "Occurrence, Distribution and Functional Significance of Taste Buds in Lizards," *Copeia*, 1985(1): 91-101.

Siebenrock, F. (1893) "Das Skelett von *Brookesia superciliaris* Kuhl," *Sber. Akad. Wiss.*, Wien, 102: 71-118.

Steffen, D. & K. Steffen (1989) MS. *Terrarienbau,* Kamen.

Stettler, P.H. (1973) *Handbuch der Terrarienkunde.* Kosmos Verlag, Stuttgart.

Tamm, K., V. Müller & W. Schmidt (1988) "Haltung und Zucht von *Furcifer cephalolepis*," *Herpetofauna*, 10(57): 11-14.

Wager, V. A. (1981) *The Life of Chameleon. A Wildlife Handbook.*

Werner, F. (1902) "Prodomus einer Monographie der "Chamäleonten," *Zool. Ib. Syst.*, 15: 295-460.

Werner, F. (1911) Chamaeleontidae," *Das Tierreich,* 27: 1-52.

Werner, F. (1912) "Das Bodenbewohnen des Chamäleons," *Bl. Aquar. Terrarienk*, 40: 7-9.

Witte, G.-Fr. (1965) "Les Chaméléons de l'Afrique Centrale," *Mus. R. Afr. Cent.*, Tervuren, Belg. Ann., Ser. 8°, Sci. Zool., 142: 1-215.

Zimmerman, E. (1983) *Das Züchten von Terrarientieren.* Kosmos Verlag, Stuttgart. (1986b. *Reptiles and Amphibians. Care, Behavior, Reproduction.* T.F.H. Publ.; Neptune, NJ.)